Nature's Children

ALLIGATORS

Melanie Zola
and
Katherine Grier

 Grolier

FACTS IN BRIEF

Classification of the American alligator
   Class: *Reptilia* (reptiles)
   Order: *Crocodilia* (crocodilians)
   Family: *Crocodylidae* (crocodile family)
   Genus: *Alligator*
   Species: *Alligator mississippiensis*

World distribution.   Exclusive to the United States; closely related to the caimans of South and Central America; other species in this genus is the Chinese Alligator, found in the Yangtze River region of China.

Habitat.   Edges of lakes, swamps and rivers.

Distinctive physical characteristics.   Black or dark gray skin; short legs and large powerful tail; eyes, ears and nostrils located on upper surface of broad head.

Habits.   Solitary; hibernates in cold weather in burrows it digs; female buries eggs in a mud nest and guards them.

Diet.   Fish, small animals and birds.

Published originally as
"Getting to Know . . . Nature's Children."

This series is approved and recommended by the Federation of Ontario Naturalists.

Canadian Cataloguing in Publication Data

Zola, Melanie, 1952–
   Alligators

(Nature's children)
Includes index.
ISBN 0-7172-1906-2 (bound) — ISBN 0-7172-2763-4 (pbk.)

1. Alligators—Juvenile literature.
I. Grier, Katherine.   II. Title.   III. Series.

QL666.C925Z64   1985   j597.98   C85-098700-8

Paperback:
Cover design: Tania Craan
Cover photo: Bachmann/
                     Hot Shots,
                     Toronto

Casebound:
Cover Photo: Stephen J.
                     Krasemann/
                     Valan Photos

Contents

Have you ever seen an alligator swimming? If you have, you might have thought that its long, tapered body and rough bark-like skin looked a lot like a floating log. Or maybe its toothy jaws and armored scales reminded you of the dinosaurs that disappeared from the earth long ago.

For many years most people judged alligators by how they looked or by frightening stories other people told. Alligators seemed like monsters from the swamps. In some stories, they even breathed fire and smoke.

It is not easy to watch alligators in the wild: they are shy and good at hiding. But gradually naturalists have begun to sort the facts from the stories. They have found that alligators are not so different from other animals as they might seem. And like all living creatures, alligators are beautifully suited to play their own important part in the natural world.

The American Alligator is the largest reptile in North America.

Just What Are Alligators?

The Spanish were the first Europeans to explore the American south, where the American Alligator lives. They called the alligator "el lagarto," which means "giant lizard." (Run the Spanish words together and you will see where the name "alligator" comes from.)

But alligators are not really lizards at all. They are crocodilians. Their only close relatives are the crocodiles, the caimans of South and Central America and the gavial, which lives in India.

The Spanish had the right idea, however, because both crocodilians and lizards are reptiles.

Like other reptiles, alligators have tough, scaly skin, breathe air into their lungs and are cold-blooded. "Cold-blooded" does not mean that their blood is cold. It just means that the temperature around them affects their body temperature. They become warmer as the temperature outside rises and cooler as it falls.

Caimans are more closely related to alligators than crocodiles are. They are not native to North America, but, the Spectacled Caiman, seen here, has been introduced and seems to be establishing itself in southern Florida.

Crocodilian Who's Who

People often get the alligator and the crocodile mixed up. And, in fact, it can be difficult to look at one and be sure which it is. If you saw both together, however, it would be easier.

Alligator

The alligator has a broad, blunt snout. The crocodile, on the other hand, has a rather narrow snout that comes to more of a point at the tip. Also, in crocodiles the upper and lower teeth are more or less in line, and the large fourth lower tooth fits into a notch in the upper jaw. As a result this tooth remains visible even when the animal's mouth is closed. The alligator's lower teeth close inside the upper ones, and the large fourth lower tooth fits into a pit in the upper jaw. It cannot be seen when the alligator's mouth is closed.

Crocodile

Apart from these visible differences, there are differences of location and behavior. Crocodiles live only in the tropics. The only place they and alligators are found together is in the southernmost part of Florida. Finally alligators are less aggressive and they move more slowly than their crocodile relatives.

Alligator Country

Because alligators are cold-blooded, they cannot survive where the winters are very cold. In spite of this, they live much farther north than most of their crocodilian relatives.

The Chinese Alligator lives in the Yangtze River Valley in China, and the American Alligator can be found almost halfway up the east coast of the United States.

Where alligators live in North America.

Wet Homes

Alligators usually live in fresh water, but sometimes they are seen where fresh and salt water mix, at places where inland rivers or marshes meet the ocean. They prefer slow water to fast-moving water. And they avoid muddy water because it is hard to see and catch prey in the dark murkiness.

Alligators find slow, fresh, clear water in many places—in swamps, marshes, streams, lagoons, even in places where many small ponds lie close together.

Wherever they live, alligators are creatures of the shallows and shores. There they find their food. And there they find the conditions that help their bodies stay at a comfortable temperature.

A Thick Skin

The alligator's tough, blackish skin protects it from the roughness of the ground. Long ago, in the age of the dinosaurs, it probably also protected the alligator's ancestors from large enemies. Today those enemies no longer exist.

The alligator's skin is made up of rectangular scales. They run down its body in rows and are joined by narrow bands of heavy, wrinkled skin. The large scales on the alligator's back and neck look like armor. They rise into ridges in the center and are strengthened inside with small plates of bone. The scales on the alligator's belly are also tough. But they are smooth and flat, and they do not have bony plates inside them.

A rest in the sun.

On the Move

Opposite page:

"Do I smell dinner?"

An alligator's legs are short and its body is long and heavy. It looks as if it should be clumsy and slow.

But in the water, the alligator is graceful and fast. The alligator uses its short legs and webbed feet to steady itself in the water—just as you use your hands and arms to steady yourself when you float. To swim, it tucks its feet close to its body and sweeps its flat, heavy tail from side to side. At top speed, an alligator can move through the water much faster than a person paddling a canoe.

On land, the alligator is not quite as graceful. It can run quickly for short distances, but it tires quickly and must stop to rest. Even so, an alligator sometimes travels long distances overland to find a new home.

When an alligator walks, its short legs hold its body off the ground, but its tail drags along behind.

Under Water

When you swim underwater do you use a mask and snorkel? An alligator does not need to wear any special equipment. Its underwater equipment is built in!

To keep the water out of its eyes, the alligator has an extra eyelid which slides sideways over its eyes. The eyelid is clear so the alligator can see through it. Flaps of skin automatically close over the alligator's slit-like ears when it dives. And a system of muscles and fleshy flaps around the nostrils controls the intake of air and water so that it never accidentally gets a noseful or lungful.

Because alligators need to breathe in air through their noses, they have come up with a way of keeping their nose out of the water even when the rest of them is almost totally submerged. They have their nostrils high on the tip of their snouts. Sometimes all you can see when an alligator is swimming is the tip of its nose and its eyes.

Opposite page:

Danger lurks in the swamp for any unwary animal.

A Meaty Diet

Alligators are meat eaters. The kind of meat alligators eat depends on where they live. An alligator that lives on a riverbank will not find the same prey as one in a swamp or marsh.

Some of the alligator's prey live in the water—slow-moving fish, turtles and frogs. Some, such as water birds and snakes, swim or dive into the water to look for food. And others, such as muskrats, rabbits, young deer and raccoons, share the banks or shore with the alligator or come to the water's edge to drink. Very large alligators will even attack cows.

Alligators also swallow hard objects. No one is quite sure why, but some naturalists think that swallowed rocks or bones or chunks of wood help grind up the alligator's food. Others think that their weight helps the alligator keep its balance in the water.

Hunting by Surprise

Most of the time, an alligator does not travel very far to hunt. Instead it lies in one place, still and hidden, waiting to catch its prey by surprise. And it can hide very well. Its dark, rough body looks like a log. And as we have discovered, its nostrils and eyes are often the only things that show above the water.

No one is quite sure how an alligator first senses its prey—by smelling it, seeing it or feeling the vibrations its movements make. If its prey is not close enough to catch, the alligator stalks stealthily closer and closer. When its prey is within reach, it lunges forward and seizes it with a sideways snap of its jaws. If the prey puts up a fight, the alligator may pull it underwater and hold it there until it drowns.

An alligator swims by sweeping its tail from side to side.

What a Mouthful

The alligator's jaws are ideal for grabbing and holding. They are lined with large, cone-shaped teeth. And powerful muscles snap them shut. But the alligator's pointed teeth are not well suited for chewing. Most of the time the alligator swallows its prey whole. If a catch is too big, it tears it into pieces that are small enough to swallow.

Alligators do not use up the energy in food as quickly as many other animals. This means they do not need to eat as much as you might expect. Sometimes an alligator will make a catch just because it is easy. Then it might hold the meal in its mouth for hours before feeling hungry enough to swallow.

Jaws!

Trespassers Beware!

Each alligator has its own territory—a piece of land and water that it and no other adult alligator will consider its own. A younger alligator may have to seek a new and bigger territory several times as it grows larger and stronger. A full-grown one may use the same territory year after year.

Alligators rarely fight over territory. Instead they have safer ways of avoiding or settling arguments. By closing their mouth and forcing air out their nostrils, they make a deep roaring sound. When an alligator bellows over and over again from the same place, it is saying: "This place is already taken."

If an alligator enters an occupied territory, the owner lunges toward the intruder, hissing loudly and open-mouthed. Although the owner is putting on a show and not a real attack, the intruder usually leaves.

Staying Warm and Keeping Cool

An alligator spends much of its time keeping warm, but not too warm. It often spends the night in the water since the water has been warmed by the heat of the sun. By dawn, the night air will have cooled the water off. Then the alligator climbs out and warms itself in the sun on the shore.

When it gets too hot, an alligator cannot cool itself by sweating as you can. Instead it opens its jaws to let heat escape through the moist lining of its mouth. Or it finds a shady resting place in the water.

Alligators and puppy dogs may not seem to have much in common, but both pant to cool themselves off.

Coping with Winter

Alligators cannot survive cold northern winters, but some do live where the winters get very chilly. How do they manage?

In the early autumn, they dig shelters. Some clear a shelter among the roots at the edge of a river bank; others dig long, narrow tunnels into soft wet banks.

There the alligator spends the coldest months of the year. Its heart beats slowly, and its body uses up its food so slowly that it eats very little or nothing. Often it does not stir until warm weather returns.

On a warm winter day an alligator may venture out of its den to bask in the sun.

Staying Wet in the Dry Season

Alligators who live farther south do not have to worry about cold. Instead they must guard against the dry weather that winter sometimes brings. Dry weather may make the water level in their home pond or river drop. When this happens, the alligators may not be able to find enough food. How do alligators survive a dry spell?

While the water is still high from summer rains, they use their tails and bodies to wallow out and deepen part of their pond or marsh. They sweep the dark muck up from the bottom to make a round rim just below the water's surface. When the shallower water dries up, water is still left in the deeper "gator-hole." During the dry season, gator-holes become the center of life not only for the alligator. Many other creatures find them handy places to live and find food and drink.

Because water is slower to chill than air, the gator-hole also gives the alligator some protection against an unexpected cold spell.

Two lovestruck alligators.

Spring Mating

Spring is mating time for alligators. Naturalists are not sure how male and female alligators find one another. Some think they leave trails of scent on the ground which other alligators can follow. Both males and females seem to search for a mate, and if several males find one female, the female seems to do the choosing.

Once the female has chosen, the male follows her about, strokes her back and sometimes blows bubbles past her snout. After 3 to 17 days, the female is ready to mate. She lets the male fertilize the eggs she is carrying inside her. Now the eggs can develop into baby alligators. After the adults mate, they have nothing more to do with one another.

Building a Nest

In early June, about two months after mating, the female gets ready to build a nest.

She usually chooses a partly shady spot close to the water. The nest must be cool enough so that the eggs will not overheat and high enough that flood waters cannot reach them.

Using her body and tail, she makes a mound of earth, leaves and grasses. She works mostly at night, resting now and then. After several nights, she has built a mound about one metre (3 feet) wide and about as high as your thigh. She packs the mound down by crawling all over it. Finally she uses her hind feet to dig a hole in the top.

When the nest is ready, she lays her eggs in the hole at the top. Fully grown females may lay as many as 52 eggs, but most lay about 30. The eggs are bright white, the same shape at both ends and almost twice the size of a chicken egg.

When all the eggs are laid, the female carefully covers over the hole to keep the eggs safe and warm.

Opposite page:

There's plenty of nesting material here.

A Nest to Guard

Once the eggs are laid, it takes two or three months before the baby alligators are ready to hatch.

The female guards her nest, often resting her throat against it. If she senses a threat, she tries to scare the intruder away without really fighting. She lunges and hisses the same way alligators defend their territory.

Some naturalists think that the female stays by her nest and does not even leave to eat until the young have hatched. Others think that she watches carefully at first but eventually leaves to find food.

The female alligator stays close to her nest to discourage visitors.

Happy Hatchday

Having a tough protective shell is handy for the baby alligators. It keeps them safe as they grow inside it. But getting out of that tough shell at hatchtime can be a problem. The hatchlings cut their way out of their shells using a special "egg-tooth." This is not really a tooth. It is a hard tip on the end of their snouts that falls off soon after they hatch.

How do alligators get out of their mound nest? No one seems to know for sure. Some people think that their mother hears her young grunting inside their eggs before they hatch and uncovers the nest to help them out. Others say the grunts are so faint that she cannot hear them. They think baby alligators, like newly hatched turtles, climb out of the nest on their own.

A mother alligator may use her sharp claws and teeth to pull the nest mound apart so the hatchlings can get out.

Alligator Hatchlings

If you ever saw a baby alligator you might wonder how all that alligator fit into such a small shell. A baby alligator is about 22 centimetres (9 inches) long. That is longer than a new pencil.

It is shaped exactly like its parents, except that its belly sticks out with leftover egg yolk. It will feed on this yolk for its first few days. Its undersides are dull white, its back and sides blackish with wandering white lines. Within a week, the white turns to yellow and then gradually darkens until the young alligator has its blackish adult coloring.

The first thing a baby alligator does is make its way to the safety of the water. Some think the mother leads the way. Others think the babies hatch knowing which way to go.

On its own.

Early Life

Life is hard for a baby alligator. Great blue herons, hawks and other birds of prey, some snakes and the occasional fish or bullfrog find the hatchling an easy catch.

Adult alligators share the water and shore with the hatchlings, but the only time they pay attention to a young alligator is when it cries out shrilly over and over again. This is a distress call and the young alligator uses it only when it is seized by a predator. Any adult alligator who hears it rushes to the youngster's defense.

The rest of the time, the young alligator looks after itself. It finds its own shelter and catches its own food—water insects, spiders, tadpoles, crayfish or anything else that is smaller and slower than it is.

With all the dangers, it is not surprising that only one in ten baby alligators survives its first year.

Baby alligators are busy hunters. They eat minnows, tadpoles, crabs and aquatic insects.

Growing Up

A young alligator grows quickly. In its first year it may triple in length. After that it may grow as much as 30 centimetres (12 inches) a year. Exactly how fast an alligator grows seems to depend on how well it can feed and where it lives. Young alligators in a marsh full of waterlife grow faster than young alligators in swamps or rivers where the pickings are slimmer.

When an alligator is four years old, it is a little over one metre (3 feet) long. At this age it stops making the distress call and starts answering it instead. It is not yet fully grown, however. Instead it is like a teenager in the alligator world. About this time, adults start driving it off their territory, and it must set out to find a territory of its own. It begins to practice bellowing, sounding a little raspy at first.

Next season, when it is five, the young alligator will be ready to mate for the first time.

Long Lives

Although they are ready to mate when they are five, alligators continue to grow for several more years. They grow quickly until they are about eight years old. By then they are about two and three-quarters metres (9 feet) long. After that their growth slows down. Females grow only a little bit more. Some males stop growing at about four metres (13 feet) but get broader and heavier. Others stay slim but grow even longer—up to about five metres (16 feet).

As an alligator grows, its tough outer skin is shed in tiny flakes as new skin grows in underneath. The alligator's teeth, too, are constantly being replaced, and this will continue almost all through its life. Fortunately, the alligator does not lose its worn teeth all at once, so it is never completely toothless. The different ages of an alligator's teeth explain why some are big and some are small.

After an alligator reaches four or five, it has few enemies. It may live for many years—up to 50 for males and 30 for females.

Opposite page:

See you later, alligator!

Skilled Survivors

Alligators may look and sometimes act threatening, but people have little real reason to fear them. In fact, an alligator will go out of its way to avoid people and will not knowingly attack a human being unless it is provoked or cornered. And, as we have seen, the alligator's appearance and behavior are ideally suited to its way of life as a cold-blooded reptile, hunter and swimmer.

The alligator's skill as a hunter and the incredible story of its youthful struggle to survive should win our admiration, not our fear. Let us hope that as more is known about this remarkable animal, fantastic stories will be replaced by far more interesting facts.

Words to Know

Cold-blooded   Term used for animals that have no automatic internal control of their body temperature.

Crocodilians   Family of reptiles that includes alligators and crocodiles.

Egg tooth   A hard point on the tip of a baby alligator's nose which it uses to break its way out of its shell.

Lagoon   Pond or small lake connected with a larger body of water.

Marsh   A flat area of land covered with shallow water.

Mate   To come together to produce young.

Naturalist   A person who studies nature.

Nostrils   The openings that allow air into the nose.

Predator   Animal that hunts other animals for food.

Prey   An animal hunted by another animal for food.

Reptile   Class of cold-blooded animals that includes snakes, alligators, turtles and lizards.

Scales   Thin, hard plates that form the outer layer of the alligator's skin.

INDEX

Cover Photo: Stephen J. Krasemann (Valan Photos)
Photo Credits: Stephen J. Krasemann (Valan Photos), pages 4, 15, 33; Bill Ivy, page 7; Kennon Cooke (Valan Photos), pages 8, 12; J. D. Taylor (Miller Services), page 16; Robert C. Simpson (Valan Photos), page 21; Barry Ranford, page 22; John Fowler (Valan Photos), page 25; Norman Lightfoot (Eco-Art Productions), pages 26, 37; J. D. Markou (Miller Services), page 29; C. P. George (Miller Services), page 30; Harold Lambert (Miller Services), page 34; J. A. Wilkinson (Valan Photos), page 38; Harold V. Green (Valan Photos), pages 41, 45; Guy Lebel (Valan Photos), page 42.

Printed and Bound in Italy by Lego SpA